It's Scary Sometimes

by '' I and the Others ''
Writers' Collective:

Marcella Bacigalupi
Giorgio Bini
Claudio Costantini
Piero Fossati

in collaboration with
Adriana Antolini
Lamberto Cavallin

with drawings
by the children
themselves

Translated by Linda Sartor
and Belinda Sifford

 HUMAN SCIENCES PRESS
72 Fifth Avenue   3 Henrietta Street
NEW YORK, NY 10011 ● LONDON, WC2E 8LU

Library of Congress Catalog Number 77-17641
ISBN: 0-87705-366-9
Copyright 1978 by Human Sciences Press, 72 Fifth Avenue
New York, N.Y. 10011

Printed in Italy
89   987654321

This book is a translation
of *Le Paure dei Bambini*
published in Italian
by La Ruota Editrice
Genova, 1975

Library of Congress Cataloging in Publication Data

" I and the Others " Writers' Collective.
It's Scary Sometimes.

Translation of Le paure dei bambini.
SUMMARY: Explores and explains some of the common fears of chil-
dren.
1. Fear in children—Juvenile literature. [1. Fear]
I. Bacigalupi, Marcella   II. Title.
BF723.F414   1978   152.4   77-17641
ISBN 0-87705-366-9

"I used to be scared of silence and the noises you sometimes hear in the silence and they sound like footsteps

When I go to bed I always pick up my feet because I'm scared 'they'll' get me by the feet"

There isn't anybody who's not afraid of something.
" If I have to cross the street and I see a bus coming at me, I'm afraid I'll get run over so I stop where I am."
" If I have to stick a plug in the wall I'm careful because I'm afraid of getting an electric shock."

If I'm at the top of a ladder or on a table I'm scared of falling, so I'm extra care-ul."

eing run over by a bus, getting a shock, or falling down are things we are all fraid of, grownups as well as children.

"SCARED TO DEATH, MY BROTHER DANNY TAKES THE CLOTHES OFF THE LINE WHILE STANDING ON A TABLE"

It's right to be afraid of these things because they're really dangerous.
" If I'm not afraid of anything, how can I be ready to escape from danger?
would always be taking a chance of hurting myself. If I'm not afraid of a roarin
bus and I don't get out of its way fast enough, I can be run over. "

n these cases fear protects us. Animals are sometimes afraid, too. Squirrels get scared and run away from noises that might mean danger. Mother hens hide their chicks when they sense a stranger approaching, because a stranger is unknown.

Children aren't only afraid of dangerous things.
Sometimes they're scared of the dark, or of harmless animals, or of strange
creatures like the devil, ghosts, or monsters.
They may be afraid of staying by themselves, even if they're safe at home.

Children are ashamed of being afraid. They believe that they are the only ones who are scared, and don't want the whole gang to find out.
But their playmates are just as afraid.

'' When my uncle was living with us I was really afraid to go into the dark bed-room and my uncle would say,'' Go on, there's no one there.'' And so I would go in, but I was scared and would go only as far as the first bed, but my uncle would tell me,'' Go over to the window; there's no one.'' But I wouldn't go. ''

Ellen, age 8½

'' I'm awful scared of the dark because my cousin once told me that lots of little ghosts live in the dark. Now I'm not so afraid of the dark as I was when I was littler. I used to be so scared that I always wet my bed. One day my mommy bought me a toy gun and from then on I used to carry that gun in the dark and yell out,'' Who's there? ''

Michael, age 6

" Bugs really give me the creeps. Once I saw a little dark green bug with long legs sitting in our sink. I started running around the house screaming. I'm scared of bugs because they're crawly and have long legs. »

Mark, age 5

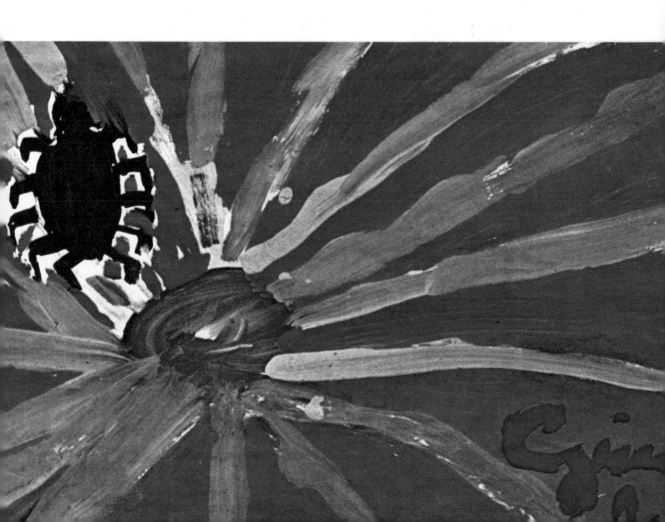

" When I'm alone I get scared so I ask myself, ' What's there to be afraid of? '
But I don't know the reasons why. At night when it's dark, those critters that
stare at me are horrible, so I keep one eye shut and the other one wide open. "

Robert, age 6

" Sometimes I dream that the darkness is squeezing me with strong, fierce
hands. "

Sonia, age 8

"When I turn on the TV at home and hear music and then I turn it off and I hear only silence, I'm afraid because I hear the silence, so I stamp my feet to hear a noise and that way it seems like there's someone there."

Lisa, age 6½

"I'm scared of being followed, because I'm afraid that in one giant leap they'll get me and then they'll tear me to pieces, skin me and roast me alive, and then they'll bury me alive."

Jim, age 7

Dogs, spiders, and the dark aren't really dangerous. The devil, ghosts, and monsters aren't dangerous either, because they're made-up things.
Why are kids afraid of them?

When kids are smaller than two years old, they don't really understand the things they see.

For example, they don't know that everything is still there after they close their eyes or when the lights are off. They are afraid of the dark because everything they are used to seeing around them "disappears."

They only feel safe if someone they know like their mother is nearby to protect them.

Little children don't know the world around them very well. They haven't had time yet to learn and discover much. Anything that is new or different can frighten them – for example, a dog or strange person. This happens mostly when grownups don't encourage kids to explore on their own.

Little by little, as children grow they learn how to tell the difference between things that are dangerous and those that aren't.
They make discoveries by playing with things, by touching them and even breaking them. That way strange things become more friendly. By the time they start school, they know that not all dogs will bite them, that certain bugs are harmless, that strangers are men and women iust like Mommy and Daddy.

But they still have many fears.
Sometimes children are afraid when someone tells them a scary story or when
they see certain kinds of movies.

Children know that these stories aren't real. They know they are only make-be-lieve.'' But why do we make up things that later make us afraid?''
To answer this question, we should understand that certain thoughts or emo-tions form inside every one of us, even when we don't realize it.

For example, all kids feel a need to play rough, to touch and break things. They might even want to beat up someone who tries to stop them from doing it. They feel angry and would like to let off steam.

But they can't.
Grownups stop that from happening.
Kids have already learned that they can't do certain things. They can't lock
Daddy out of the house just because he stops them from making noise. They'd
like to, but Daddy is stronger than they are. If anything, he can punish them.

Anger keeps building up inside and can't get out. Kids feel terrible and think they are bad.

They all have to get rid of these feelings, so they imagine that things outside them have these bad feelings. They see danger in things that aren't really dangerous, like certain animals or "pretend" creatures.

In this way they take the danger out of themselves.

But then they're afraid.

Kids need grownups because they need protection and help. If adults overpro-
tect them, however, kids feel small and helpless in comparison.
They get madder and their anger grows.
Their fears grow, too.

It's hard to get rid of fears completely. But they can be limited by letting chi
dren be freer to move around, touch things, make discoveries. This depend
partly on parents' personalities as well as how much money they have an
where they live. For example, if kids don't have their own area to play in, there'
a much greater chance they'll break something, and if parents don't hav
enough money to replace these things, they'll probably get VERY angry.

Sometimes kids just need a little attention to eliminate their fears, but parents can't always give this to them. Mommy and Daddy are really tired when they come home. They've been working hours and hours, often at hard, boring jobs. Of course, they'd rather do things that are more fun, but most of them can't be-cause they have to support a family. Parents' anger builds up, too. And that means they may scream at kids for making the tiniest noise or touching the smallest thing.

Kids would have fewer fears if they had space at home and yards and parks to play in. Or if grownups weren't so exhausted that they couldn't put up with the noise children normally make. Or if daddies and mommies were never nervous or worried.

But all these " ifs " will only be possible when parents begin to worry less about the rent, prices, medical bills and work. Because families do live with these worries, we'll all have to work together to make the world an easier place to live in.

" But right now we kids still have our fears. What can we do about them? "
First, don't worry too much about them.
They'll go away little by little as you grow up.
And they'll go away even faster if grownups treat you with love and under-standing.

Many grownups nave forgotten how afraid they were as kids. They demand that their kids act just like grownups. They can't understand how kids think, and want them to think the way big people do.

"How can kids defend themselves?"
You can explain to the grownups that it's stupid and mean to make kids go
where it's dark if they're scared. If you're afraid to go to sleep in a dark room,
maybe some grownup can give up a TV program to come and keep you com-
pany.

We kids can also ask grownups to stop scaring us with stories about the de-
l, the bogey man, or the wolf.

grownups listen to us, they can really help us kids feel braver and more se-
ure. "

S. G. M. - Casale Monferr